**AUDIO ACCESS INCLUDED**
Recorded Accompaniments Online

Young Women's Edition

TEEN BROADWAY SONGS OF THE 2010s

12 SONGS FROM TEEN MUSICAL THEATRE ROLES

T0081871

PLAYBACK+
Speed • Pitch • Balance • Loop

To access audio visit:
www.halleonard.com/mylibrary

Enter Code
7127-8606-8073-9456

ISBN 978-1-5400-6022-8

HAL•LEONARD®

Visit Hal Leonard Online at
www.halleonard.com

Contact us:
Hal Leonard
7777 West Bluemound Road
Milwaukee, WI 53213
Email: info@halleonard.com

In Europe, contact:
Hal Leonard Europe Limited
42 Wigmore Street
Marylebone, London, W1U 2RN
Email: info@halleonardeurope.com

In Australia, contact:
Hal Leonard Australia Pty. Ltd.
4 Lentara Court
Cheltenham, Victoria, 3192 Australia
Email: info@halleonard.com.au

HOW TO USE HAL LEONARD ONLINE AUDIO

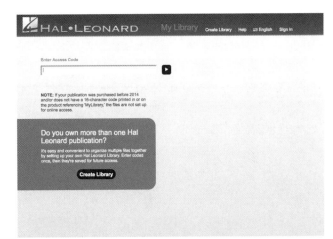

Because of the changing use of media, and the fact that fewer people are using CDs, we have made a shift to companion audio accessible online. In many cases, rather than a book with CD, we now have a book with an access code for online audio, including performances, accompaniments or diction lessons. Each copy of each book has a unique access code. We call this Hal Leonard created system "My Library." It's simple to use.

Go to www.halleonard.com/mylibrary and enter the unique access code found on page one of a relevant book/audio package.

The audio tracks can be streamed or downloaded. If you download the tracks on your computer, you can add the files to a CD or to your digital music library, and use them anywhere without being online. See below for comments about Apple and Android mobile devices.

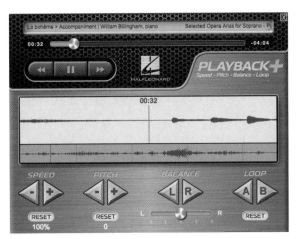

There are some great benefits to the My Library system. *Playback+* is exclusive to Hal Leonard, and when connected to the Internet with this multi-functional audio player you can:

• Change tempo without changing pitch
• Transpose to any key

Optionally, you can create a My Library account, and store all the companion audio you have purchased there. Access your account online at any time, from any device, by logging into your account at www.halleonard.com/mylibrary. Technical help may be found at www.halleonard.com/mylibrary/help/

Apple/iOS

Question: On my iPad and iPhone, the Download links just open another browser tab and play the track. How come this doesn't really download?

Answer: The Safari iOS browser will not allow you to download audio files directly in iTunes or other apps. There are several ways to work around this:

• You can download normally on your desktop computer, saving the files to iTunes. Then, you can sync your iOS device directly to your computer, or sync your iTunes content using an iCloud account.
• There are many third-party apps which allow you to download files from websites into the app's own file manager for easy retrieval and playback.

Android

Files are always downloaded to the same location, which is a folder usually called "Downloads" (this may vary slightly depending on what browser is used (Chrome, Firefox, etc)). Chrome uses a system app called "Downloads" where files can be accessed at any time. Firefox and some other browsers store downloaded files within a "Downloads" folder in the browser itself.

Recently-downloaded files can be accessed from the Notification bar; swiping down will show the downloaded files as a new "card", which you tap on to open. Opening a file depends on what apps are installed on the Android device. Audio files are opened in the device's default audio app. If a file type does not have a default app assigned to it, the Android system alerts the user.

Teen Broadway Songs of the 2010s

CONTENTS

Pianists on the recordings: [1] Brendan Fox, [2] Ruben Piirainen, [3] Richard Walters

The price of this book includes access to recorded accompaniments online, including **PLAYBACK+**, a multifunctional audio player. See access information on the title page.

ALYSSA GREENE
from *The Prom*

Lyrics by Chad Beguelin
Music by Matthew Sklar

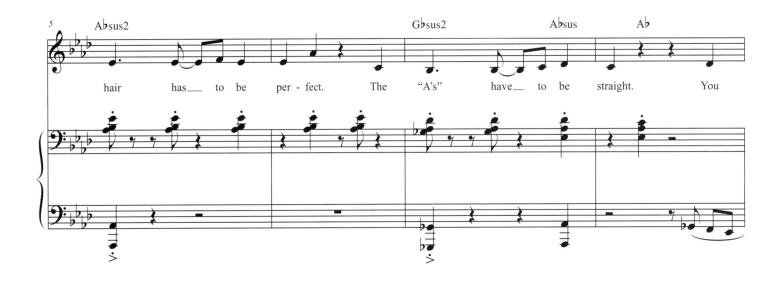

*A cut has been made for this solo edition.

HOME
from *Beetlejuice the Musical*

Words and Music by
Eddie Perfect

A Little More Energy ♩ = 146

* A cut has been made for this solo edition.
Chorus parts were eliminated.

I LOVE PLAY REHEARSAL
from *Be More Chill*

Words and Music by
Joe Iconis

CHRISTINE: Where was I? Oh, right!

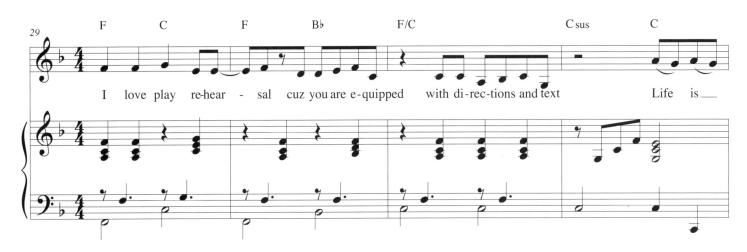

I love play re-hear - sal cuz you are e-quipped with di-rec-tions and text Life is ___

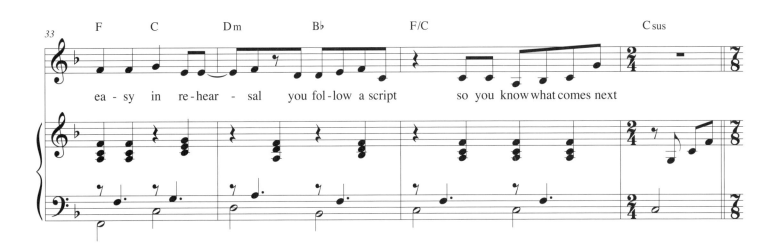

ea - sy in re-hear - sal you fol-low a script so you know what comes next

Colla Voce - SUPER FAST

An - y - hoo the point that I'm get-ting to is some-times life can't

CHRISTINE: ...that was really one of my best roles, did you see that? I was incredibly commanding, I think. It made me feel like there just aren't strong roles for women in theater these days, particularly high school theater, do you find that? Because I totally find that— [SHE SINGS]

CHRISTINE: *There's also a part of me that wants to do this. [CRAZY GOBLIN NOISE] So I did it!*

HOME
from the Broadway Musical *Wonderland*

Music by Frank Wildhorn
Lyrics by Jack Murphy

ev - er you're a - lone. That's how you know you are home. ___

___ How I wish that we could feel that, some - how,

right now. How I wish that we could feel that a - gain. ___

___ Home is like a smile you see in a pho-to-graph. No

IN MY DREAMS

from *Anastasia*

Lyrics by Lynn Ahrens
Music by Stephen Flaherty

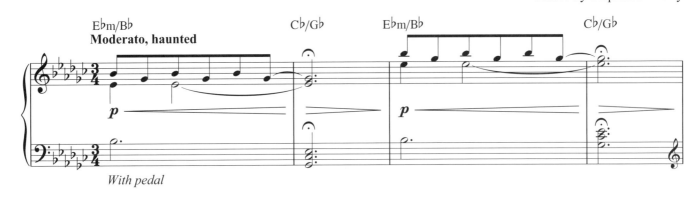

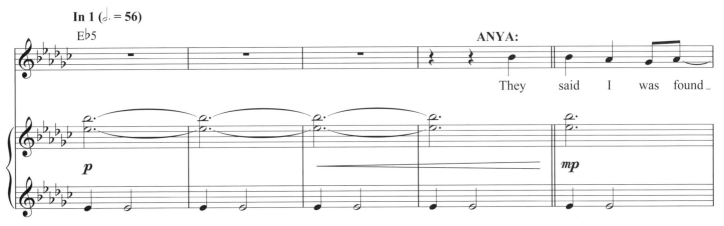

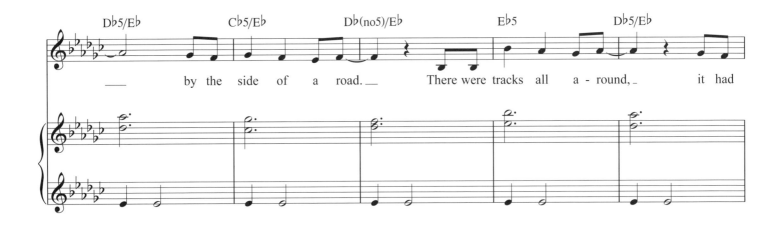

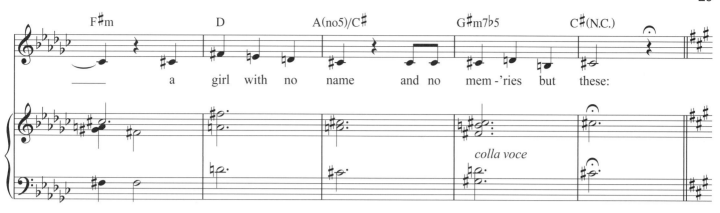

With movement

Rain a-gainst a win-dow. Sheets up-on a bed. Ter-ri-fy-ing

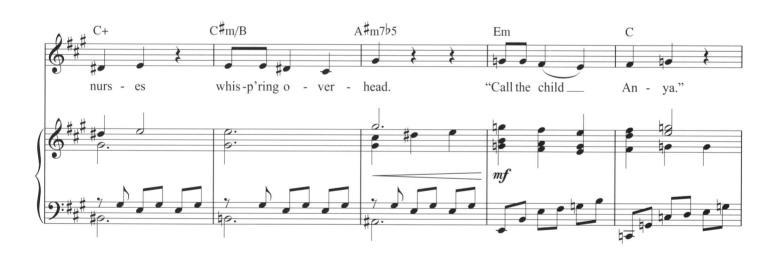

nurs-es whis-p'ring o-ver-head. "Call the child An-ya."

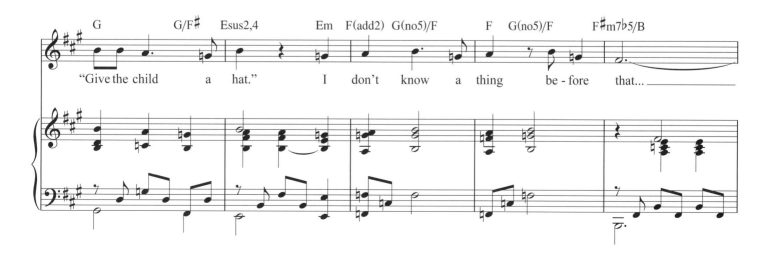

"Give the child a hat." I don't know a thing be-fore that...

JOURNEY TO THE PAST

featured in the Broadway Musical *Anastasia*

Words and Music by Lynn Ahrens
and Stephen Flaherty

Moderately (steady, not too fast) (♩ = 89)

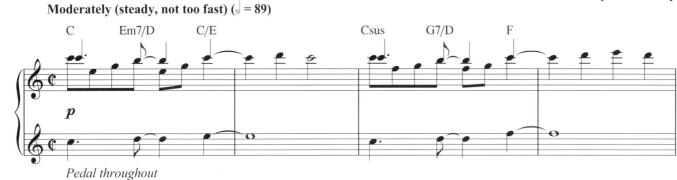

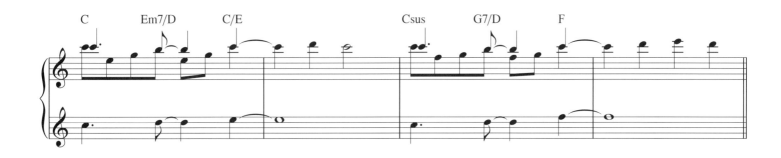

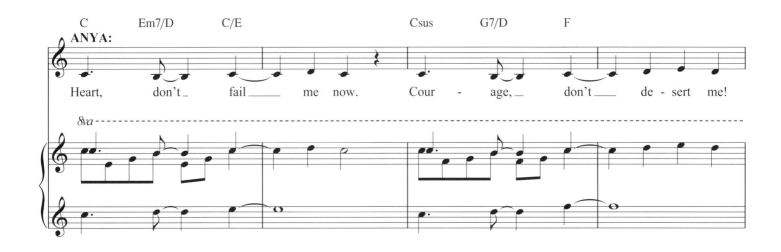

ANYA:
Heart, don't fail me now. Cour-age, don't de-sert me!

Don't turn back, now that we're here.

Lyrics:
to the past.

Home, love, fam-'ly. There was once a time I must have had them, too.

JUST BREATHE
from *The Prom*

Lyrics by Chad Beguelin
Music by Matthew Sklar

A little "Joni," in 2

ONE PERFECT MOMENT

from *Bring It On: The Musical*

Music by Tom Kitt
Lyrics by Amanda Green
and Lin-Manuel Miranda

Freely, but with slight urgency

CAMPBELL:

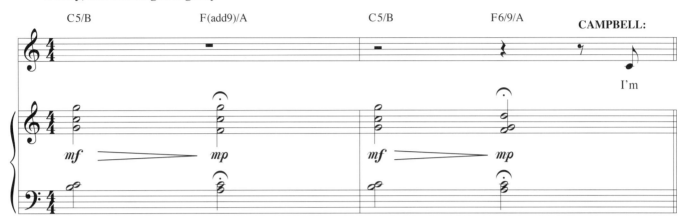

I'm

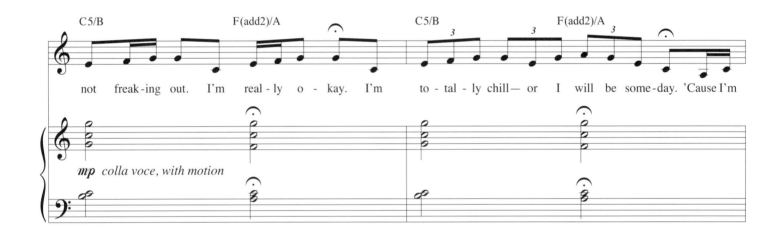

not freak-ing out. I'm real-ly o-kay. I'm to-tal-ly chill— or I will be some-day. 'Cause I'm

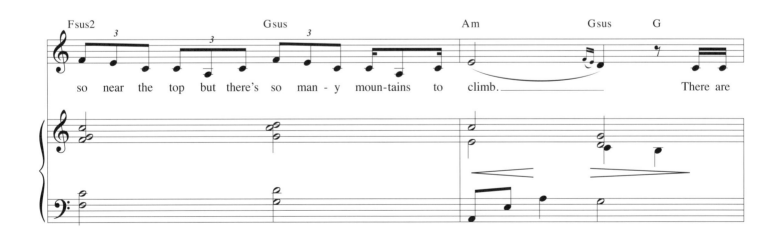

so near the top but there's so man-y moun-tains to climb. There are

plans to be planned, drills to be drilled, 'cause this dream that I dreamed is be-com-ing ful-filled— and I

plan to en-joy it but right now, I don't have the time.

With gentle movement (♩. = 59)

Fade in on Camp-bell: An av-er-age teen-ag-er, al - most grown.___

Close up on av-er-age grades from the av - er-age life she's known.___ Now

SAL TLAY KA SITI
from the Broadway Musical *The Book of Mormon*

Words and Music by Randolph Parker,
Matthew Stone and Robert Lopez

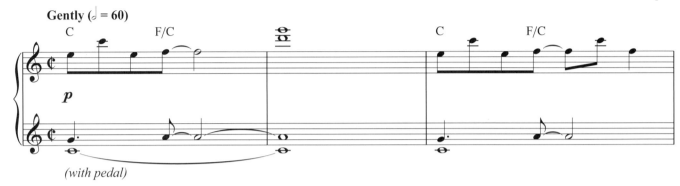

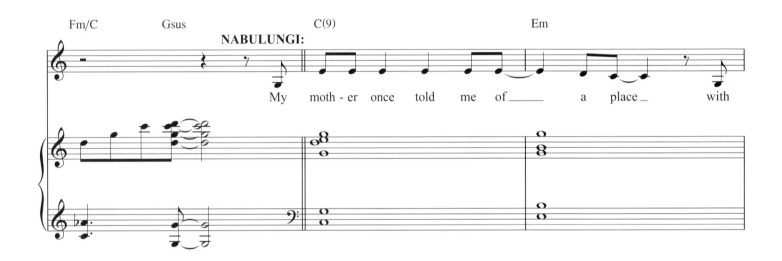

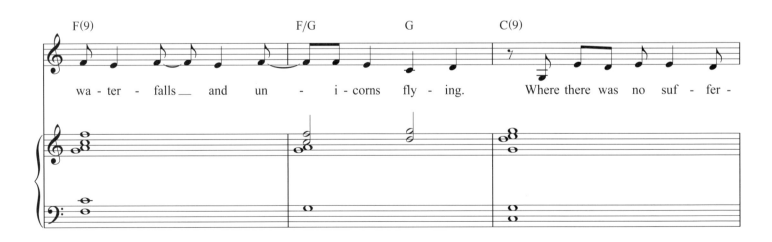

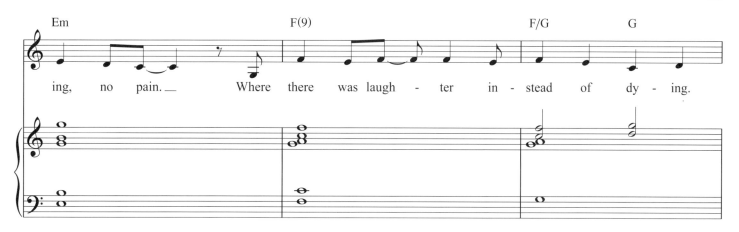

ing, no pain. __ Where there was laugh - ter in - stead of dy - ing.

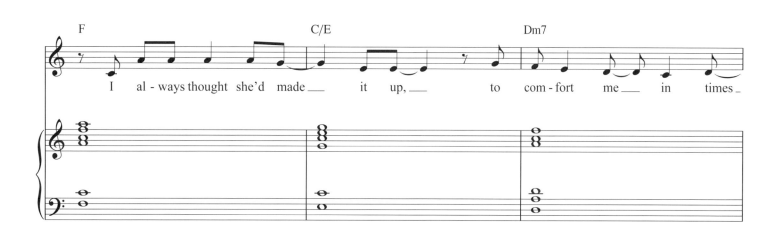

I al - ways thought she'd made __ it up, __ to com - fort me __ in times __

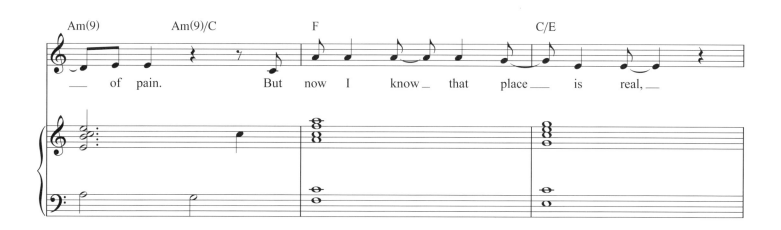

__ of pain. But now I know __ that place __ is real, __

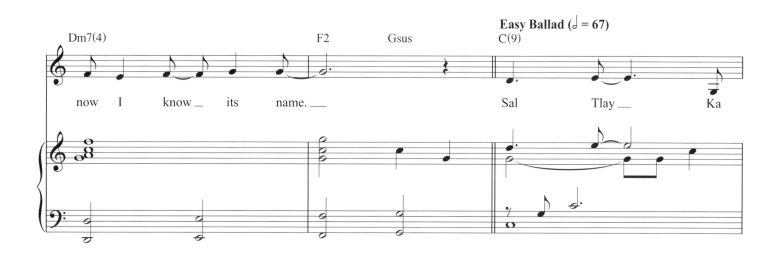

now I know __ its name. __ Sal Tlay __ Ka

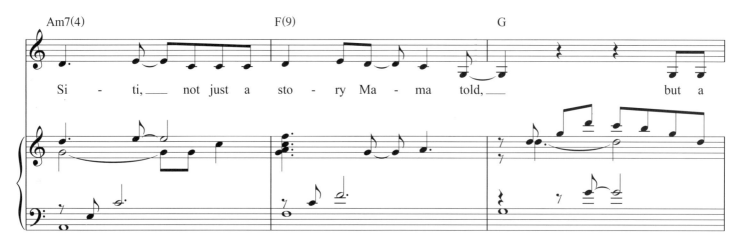

Am7(4)　　　　　　F(9)　　　　　　G

Si - ti,___ not just a sto - ry Ma - ma told,___ but a

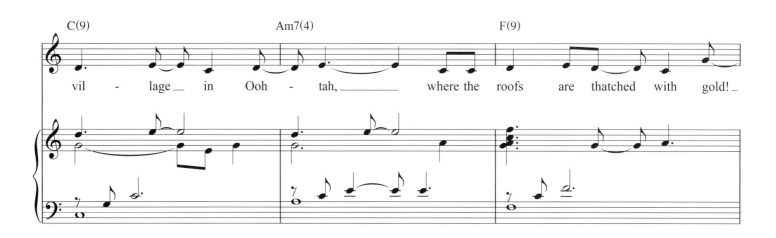

C(9)　　　　　　Am7(4)　　　　　　F(9)

vil - lage___ in Ooh - tah,_____ where the roofs are thatched with gold!_

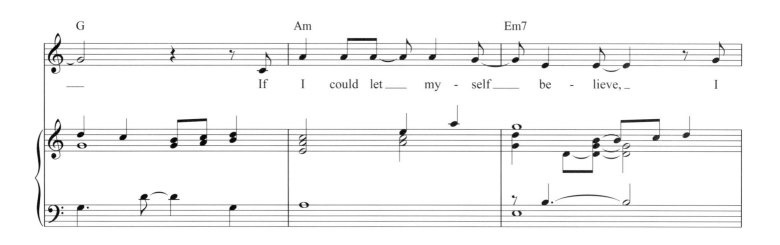

G　　　　　　Am　　　　　　Em7

___ If I could let___ my - self___ be - lieve,_ I

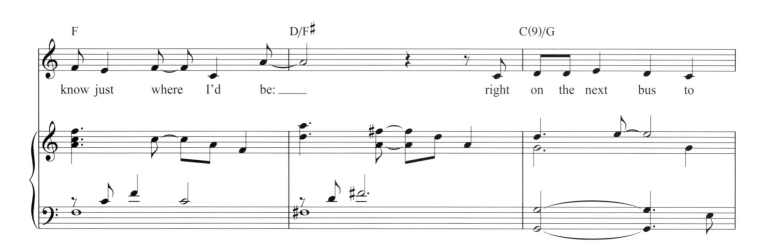

F　　　　　　D/F♯　　　　　　C(9)/G

know just where I'd be:___ right on the next bus to

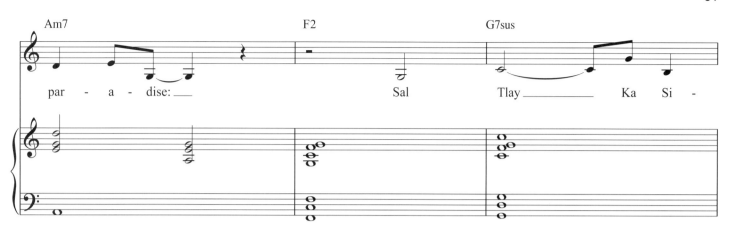

par - a - dise: ___ Sal Tlay ___ Ka Si -

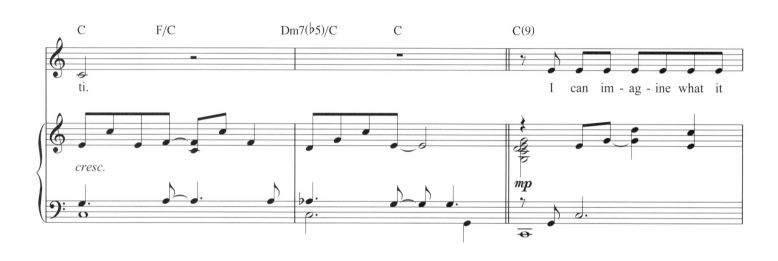

ti. I can im - ag - ine what it

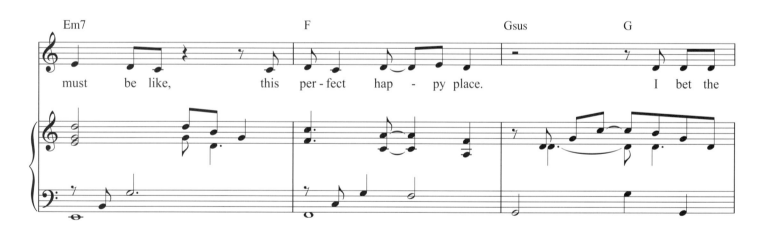

must be like, this per - fect hap - py place. I bet the

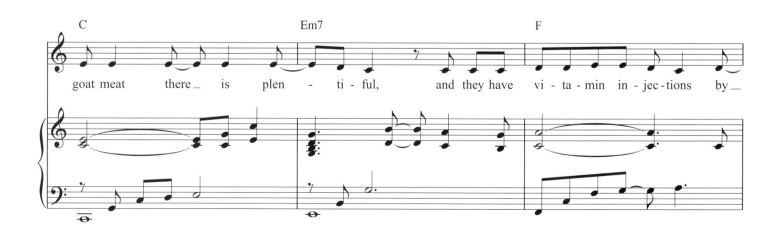

goat meat there ___ is plen - ti - ful, and they have vi - ta - min in - jec - tions by ___

the case. The war-lords there _ are friend - ly, they

help you cross _ the street. _____ And there's a Red Cross on ev - 'ry cor -

- ner, with all the flo - ur you _ can eat. _____

Sal Tlay _ Ka Si - ti, _____ the most per - fect place _ on earth. _

STUPID WITH LOVE
from *Mean Girls*

Words by Nell Benjamin
Music by Jeff Richmond

Freely

CADY: When I was five, I fell in love.— It did-n't last.

He ran— from me. Lit-er-al-ly, ran from me.— And be-ing Ken-yan, he ran— fast.

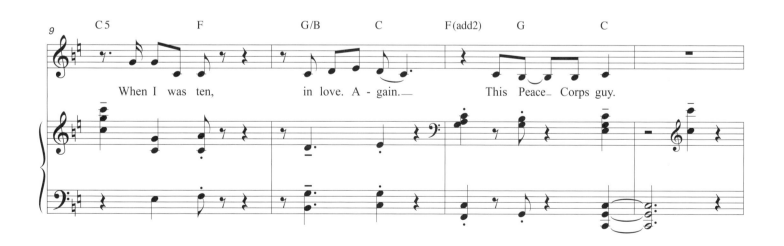

When I was ten, in love. A - gain.— This Peace— Corps guy.

WORLD BURN
from *Mean Girls*

Words by Nell Benjamin
Music by Jeff Richmond

Notch up the tempo

Ca-dy, time to watch your back.— Ca-dy, time to turn and cough.— Be-cause you took me down.

But you did-n't fin-ish me off.—

My name is Re - gi-na George. And, in case you're keep-ing score: Ca - dy may have won the bat - tle but

*A cut has been made for this solo edition.
  Chorus parts have been eliminated.

WHAT'S WRONG WITH ME?

from *Mean Girls*

Words by Nell Benjamin
Music by Jeff Richmond